ELEPHANTS

Joyce Poole

Colin Baxter Photography, Grantown-on-Spey, Scotland

ELEPHANTS

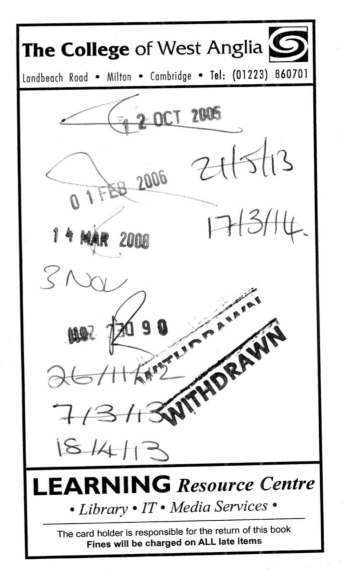

HE COLLEC

First published in Great Britain in 1997 by
Colin Baxter Photography Ltd.,
Grantown-on-Spey,
Moray PH26 3NA
Scotland

Revised edition published 2001

A CIP Catalogue record for this book is available from the British Library

ISBN 1-84107-115-3

Photographs © 1997, 2001:

Front cover © Jen & Des Bartlett (Bruce Coleman Ltd)
Back cover © Martyn Colbeck (Oxford Scientific Films)
Page 1 © Martyn Colbeck (Oxford Scientific Films)
Page 4 © Martyn Colbeck (Oxford Scientific Films)
Page 6 © Martyn Colbeck (Oxford Scientific Films)
Page 8 © Martin Harvey (NHPA)
Page 9 © Dieter & Mary Plage (Bruce Coleman Ltd)
Page 10 © Jen & Des Bartlett (Oxford Scientific Films)
Page 11 © Nigel Blake (Bruce Coleman Ltd)
Page 13 © Martyn Colbeck (Oxford Scientific Films)
Page 14 © Michael Fogden (Bruce Coleman Ltd)
Page 17 © J Zwaenepoel (Bruce Coleman Ltd)
Page 18 © Martyn Colbeck (Oxford Scientific Films)
Page 18 © Mary Plage (Bruce Coleman Ltd)
Page 21 © Stan Osolinski (Oxford Scientific Films)
Page 22 © Daryl Balfour (NHPA)
Page 25 © Martyn Colbeck (Oxford Scientific Films)
Page 26 © Gunter Ziesler (Bruce Coleman Ltd)
Page 27 © M P Khal (Bruce Coleman Ltd)
Page 29 © M P Khal (Bruce Coleman Ltd)
Page 30 © Martyn Colbeck (Oxford Scientific Films)
Page 32 © Joyce Poole

Page 33 © Martyn Colbeck (Oxford Scientific Films)
Page 34 © Martin Harvey (NHPA)
Page 37 © Daryl Balfour (NHPA)
Page 39 © Martyn Colbeck (Oxford Scientific Films)
Page 40 © Martyn Colbeck (Oxford Scientific Films)
Page 43 © Dr Hermann Brehm (Bruce Coleman Ltd)
Page 44 © John Mitchell (Oxford Scientific Films)
Page 47 © M P Khal (Bruce Coleman Ltd)
Page 48 © Steve Turner (Oxford Scientific Films)
Page 51 © M P Khal (Bruce Coleman Ltd)
Page 52 © Martin Harvey (NHPA)
Page 55 © Martyn Colbeck (Oxford Scientific Films)
Page 56 © Joyce Poole
Page 59 © Jen & Des Bartlett (Bruce Coleman Ltd)
Page 60 © Martin Harvey (NHPA)
Page 63 © Daryl Balfour (NHPA)
Page 64 © Dr Johnny Johnston (Bruce Coleman Ltd)
Page 66 © Steve Turner (Oxford Scientific Films)
Page 67 © Steve Turner (Oxford Scientific Films)
Page 69 © Martyn Colbeck (Oxford Scientific Films)
Page 70 © Stan Osolinski (Oxford Scientific Films)
Page 71 © Mary Plage (Bruce Coleman Ltd)

Printed in China

Contents

Introduction

One morning in February 1989 I was out on the Amboseli plains with Jezebel's family. The adult females were in a sleepy mid-morning sort of mood. At their feet the youngsters played their favorite game, King of the Castle. A juvenile female lay on her side wriggling her large gray body and flopping her trunk about while several babies attempted to clamber on top of her. Joshua, Joyce's teenage son, was much too old for this juvenile game of wiggling, but still too young and energetic to feel sleepy, and he came over to see what I was doing instead. I was sitting on the hood of my car taking photographs and, as he approached, I rumbled softly to him. He raised his trunk high in the air, taking in all the scents that belonged to me, and came closer. I, too, was in the mood for a game. I took off one of my old rubber flip-flops and tossed it to him. He reached his trunk tentatively toward the shoe, relaxed and elongated it, hesitated, and then swung his trunk toward my shoe again, sniffing it over and over until he decided it was safe to touch. He stretched his trunk out to its full length and picked up the flip-flop. So began our game.

Joshua had not met a flip-flop before, and so it required detailed investigation involving prolonged contact with various parts of his body. He grasped it firmly with his trunk and first stabbed it with the tip of his tusk, and then used it to scratch the underside of his trunk, which made a lovely rasping sound against the ridges of thick elephant skin. Finally he put it in his mouth and carefully chewed it, turning it slowly over and over with his large tongue. After several minutes of such examination he tossed the shoe up in the air behind him. Listening carefully to where it fell, he opened and closed his eyes as if considering the interesting new sound that it had made and then, waggling his head in an indication of amusement, he reversed several steps and

A newborn calf is helped to its feet by its mother and other family members.

reached back to touch it gently with his hind foot. Having touched it carefully from all angles and with both hind feet, he stepped firmly on it, scuffed it through the dust, stepped on it again, and then, with his back legs crossed casually, he contemplated the flip-flop in deep elephant silence.

When we humans contemplate an object, we look at it intently. Elephants take it in sensually. Joshua stood quietly, facing away from the flip-flop, perhaps reliving the wonderful new feelings he had experienced. Then he reversed further, reached back with his trunk, picked up the flip-flop, and started the game all over again. Finally, he tossed my shoe, under-trunk, back toward me. I picked my shoe off the ground, found it undamaged, and threw it back to him. We did this a couple of times until something else caught my attention, and I looked away for a minute. The next thing I knew something hard landed on my head and

An Asian elephant uses its trunk as a snorkle.

fell to the ground with a thud. Joshua had found a small piece of wildebeest bone and had thrown it at me with surprising accuracy. Joshua, a wild elephant, had understood and was entertained by our game: there we were, two species out on the plains playing catch.

Elephants are the earth's largest land mammal. Their massive size and extraordinary appearance are awe-inspiring. Those who have had a chance to watch their behavior in the wild are struck by their strong family bonds and by the tenderness with which elephants care for their young.

Elephants clear away floating vegetation before sucking water into their trunks.

*This African elephant family consists of three adult females and six immature
offspring. Young calves remain close to their mother's side and suckle until they are four or five years old.
Families are characterized by close social bonds. Family members defend one another in times of danger and show strong
affiliative behavior. Females will remain with their family for life, while males will depart at around 14 years old.*

I have had the privilege of spending 14 years in Amboseli National Park in southern Kenya studying the sexual behavior and vocal communication of African elephants. Now (2001) in its 29th year, the Amboseli Elephant Research Project, directed by Cynthia Moss, is the longest and most detailed study of wild elephants anywhere in the world. The population's 1120 elephants are each known individually, and their family histories and relationships are recorded in detail. Along with my colleagues, I have had

the unusual opportunity to know elephants as individuals with unique characters.

It is not only their size that sets elephants apart from most other animals, but their social complexity, intelligence, range and intensity of expression, and their understanding of death. After all this time, I still find myself with so many unanswered questions about these amazing creatures. On many occasions

Elephants detect scents we cannot smell and voices we cannot hear.

I have watched the excited greeting ceremony of related elephants: massive bodies spinning around urinating and defecating, temporal glands streaming, and a cacophony of ear-splitting trumpets, roars, screams and rumbles. Each time I wonder whether this display is simply a message to other elephants that the family is, once more, a force to be reckoned with or whether the elephants are actually expressing their joy at being together again. I have witnessed the intense excitement displayed by elephants at the birth of a baby, as ten, perhaps 20 elephants vocalize in chorus, their calls extraordinarily powerful, some well below the level of human hearing, reaching over 106 decibels, and traveling 3 to 6 miles (5 to 10 km). These scenes are typical of elephants during moments of social excitement; a greeting, a birth, a mating, for example. What is the function of this phenomenal chorus of calls? Are specific messages being transmitted to other elephants, or are they, as humans would be, simply overcome by the excitement of the occasion?

I have watched a female elephant die and observed other elephants spend close to an hour trying to raise her. And I have witnessed, two days later, the same elephants return to visit her butchered carcass. They stood in ghastly silence as they touched repeatedly her bloodied face where her tusks had been removed with an axe. Why did they come back? What thoughts, if any, did they have? I have observed a mother, her facial expression one I could recognize as grief, stand beside her stillborn baby for three days, and I have been moved deeply by the eerie silence of an elephant family as, for an hour, they fondled the bones of their matriarch. What were these elephants actually feeling? Was their 'grief', their 'mourning' in any way similar to our own?

I have played silly trumpeting games with young wild elephants and they have shown, by their facial expressions, that they remembered our game over two years later. What were they thinking as they walked past my car, waggling their heads and ears at me, their mouths pulled back in what appeared to be a 'smile'? I have had elephants gather in calm silence around my car to listen to my singing. Did they enjoy the melody? Whatever the answers to these questions, I am sure that the more we learn about elephants the fainter the line we have drawn between man and other animals will become. But time is running out for the elephants. If we can't find a way to accommodate one of the earth's most magnificent creatures, what possible hope is there for the myriad other less significant animals? What hope is there for us?

Elephants have favorite scratching trees and the bark is worn smooth from years of use.

Origins

Elephants belong to the larger group or order of mammals called the Proboscidea, so named after their most notable organ – the proboscis, or trunk. The Proboscideans include 353 recognized species of which 351 are now extinct; the African elephant, *Loxodonta africana*, and the Asian elephant, *Elephas maximus*, are the sole survivors of an extensive radiation which began their differentiation over 60 million years ago.

There is a wealth of information to show that Proboscidea and the Sirenia (the manatee and dugong) share a common aquatic ancestor. Palaeontological findings as well as more recent immunological, molecular and embryological evidence all point to an extremely close affinity between present-day elephants and the aquatic Sirenia. The Proboscideans' long and spectacular evolutionary history probably originated in North America with a creature named *Phosphatherium esculliei,* which lived in the late Cretaceous some 62 million years ago in what is present-day Morocco. *Phosphatherium* was about the size of a dog and, lacking a trunk, did not look anything like a modern elephant. Its teeth, however, were distinctly elephantine and looked almost identical to the next closest elephant forebear, *Moeritherium lyonsi. Moeritherium* was a small, aquatic, pig-sized creature, which possessed neither tusks nor trunk, although both its upper and lower jaws contained elongated teeth. This elephant ancestor lived in north-east Africa during the early Eocene epoch, and into the Oligocene epoch, about 50–35 million years ago.

Also living in north-east Africa some 40 million years ago were *Palaeomastodon* and *Phiomia*, large mammals which possessed tusks in both the upper and lower jaws. Their most distinctive features were strong and

Elephants use their excellent spatial memory to locate water in the arid Namibian Bush.

elongated lips and jaws which enabled them to feed by grasping leaves and grasses. *Palaeomastodon*, in particular, showed the closest beginnings of a trunk, and stood about 6.5 ft (2 m) at the shoulder. It is likely that these four mammals, *Phosphatherium*, *Moeritherium*, *Palaeomastodon* and *Phiomia*, made up the basic stock from which all other elephant-like creatures evolved.

By the Miocene, some 35 million years ago, a host of Proboscideans had radiated from Africa to Europe, Asia and North America, and among them were the deinotheres. *Deinotherium* ('terrible beast') was a massive animal, almost the size of contemporary elephants, with large tusks which came from the lower jaw and turned sharply downward so that their tips faced almost backward. It has been surmised that these were used for raking submerged vegetation from the bottom of swamps. The highly successful deinotheres survived until comparatively recently, becoming extinct only 2–3 million years ago.

Another very successful group of Proboscideans included the gomphotheres and their allies, a widespread group whose remains have been discovered in Miocene deposits in Africa, Asia, Europe and North America. The Gomphotheriidae were nearly as large as an Asian elephant with two pairs of tusks, one pair in the upper jaw and one in the lower jaw. Based on the position of the external nasal opening, the short neck and long limbs, it is speculated that *Gomphotherium* had a well developed trunk.

The family Elephantidae began with *Stegotetrabelodon* and *Stegodibelodon*, primitive forms restricted to Africa in the late Miocene and early Pliocene. These two genera lived in a mixed forest and savannah environment. Although they were similar to modern elephants in a host of ways, there were some important differences relating to the shape of their teeth, and the presence of incisors in the lower jaw.

Stegotetrabelodon gave rise to *Primelephas* which lived in open wooded savannah in east and central Africa about 6–7 million years ago. *Primelephas* stood as tall as a female African elephant and had two pairs of tusks protruding

Asian elephants are more closely related to the
extinct mammoths than they are to African elephants.

African and Asian elephants may be distinguished easily. African elephants are the larger species; they have bigger ears and a concave-shaped back. Asian elephants have smaller ears, a convex-shaped back and a large domed forehead.

forward, the upper pair over 3 ft (1 m) long, and the lower pair much shorter. *Primelephas* became the basic stock for three genera of elephants. First was the rather primitive *Loxodonta* which contains two species, one of which survives today as the African elephant. A second branch was the more progressive *Elephas*, including 11 species of which only one survives today as the Asian elephant. A third branch contained the mammoths, genus *Mammuthus*.

Fossil mammoth remains have been found in Africa, Eurasia, and North America. Perhaps the best known member of this genus was the woolly mammoth, *Mammuthus primigenius*, which survived until the very end of the Ice Age in the far northern hemisphere. The mammoth was contemporary with modern humans and numerous paintings have been found of this species in caves in Europe. In addition, frozen well-preserved carcasses have been found in Siberia and Alaska, which provide extraordinary detail of the anatomy of these creatures. Their bodies were covered with long hair and dense underwool and their tusks were long, curving first outward and then inward.

These Proboscideans, *Stegodibelodon*, *Stegotetrabelodon*, *Primelephas*, *Loxodonta*, *Elephas*, and *Mammuthus*, together make up the family Elephantidae. All members of the family, living and extinct, possess a well developed trunk. Fossil specimens of Elephantidae have been found in Africa, Europe, Asia, North America and Central America.

The African elephant, *Loxodonta africana*, and the Asian elephant, *Elephas maximus*, are the only living representatives of the family. In prehistoric times the African elephant was found throughout the African continent, but never beyond, while the Asian elephant originated in Africa and then migrated to Europe and Asia.

The most obvious superficial difference between African and Asian elephants is the size of the ears: the African elephant has very large ears, while the Asian elephant has smaller ears. People enjoy pointing out that the ear of an African elephant is shaped like the continent of Africa, while the Asian elephant's ear is shaped like the Indian sub continent. Another obvious difference is the shape of the back: the African elephant's is concave in shape, while the Asian elephant's is convex, hence its name, *Elephas maximus*, or huge arch ('ele' from the Greek meaning arch, 'phant' meaning huge, and 'maximus' meaning large from the Latin maxima). The highest body point of an African elephant is its shoulder, while the Asian elephant's highest point is the top of its head, which, unlike its cousin's, is twin-domed. African elephants are significantly less hairy than Asian elephants, probably because the latter is more closely related to the woolly mammoth. The African elephant has two finger-like tips at the end of its trunk, while the Asian elephant has only one. Another less obvious difference to the casual observer is the shape of the chewing surfaces of the teeth. The tooth plates of an African elephant are composed of lozenge-shaped enamel loops, hence its name, *Loxodonta africana*, 'lox' meaning lozenge, and 'odon' referring to tooth. The plates on a tooth of an Asian elephant, however, are closed compressed loops.

The Asian has been subdivided into three subspecies: *Elephas maximus maximus* is found on Sri Lanka; *Elephas maximus indicus* is found in peninsular India and throughout South-east Asia; and *Elephas maximus sumatranus*, the smallest of the three, is found on Sumatra and Borneo.

In Africa, two subspecies have long been recognized: the savannah or bush elephant, *Loxodonta africana africana*, and the forest elephant, *Loxodonta africana cyclotis*. The forest elephant is smaller in body size, possesses smaller, more rounded ears and generally straighter, more downward-pointing tusks than does the savannah elephant. Recent genetic work, however, suggests that there is a third subspecies, the desert elephant of Namibia, and that these linages may have diverged millions of years ago.

An Asian elephant tosses dust over his back.

THE COLLEGE OF WEST ANGLIA

The Largest of Land Mammals

African and Asian elephants share a long list of traits that are unusual among mammals, the most obvious being the possession of a trunk, a massive body, large ears, elongated incisors made of ivory, and thick skin (hence the term 'pachydermous'). Other characteristics shared by both species include their sparsely distributed body hair, the location of the external genitalia of both males and females between the hind legs, the lungs attached to the diaphragm, a heart with a double-pointed apex (instead of a typical one-point mammalian heart), two anterior vena cavae, the lack of a gall bladder, and the testes located inside the abdomen near the kidneys. The elephants are different in so many respects from other mammals that a review of their anatomy and physiology is fascinating.

Elephants are the largest living land mammals and sexual dimorphism (morphological differences between males and females) in body size is extreme. Females begin approaching a plateau in height and weight growth in their late twenties, while males continue to grow through most of their lives, eventually reaching twice the weight of adult females. Among African elephants, fully grown males may attain over 13,000 lb (6000 kg) while females reach only half that weight. By the time an African male elephant reaches sexual maturity, at about 17 years old, his shoulder height exceeds that of a fully grown female. Yet at this size he is still a mere teenager. He is only 80% of his full adult height and a little over half his full adult weight; he cannot begin to compete with older males for mates. Unlike most other mammals, elephants continue to grow in body size long after puberty. The ability of elephants to continue growing in height beyond the age of sexual maturity is related to the unusual delayed epiphyseal fusion of the long bones, a pattern more pronounced in males than in females. The epiphyses are a part of the bone that ossifies separately from the

Elephants are gray, but mud comes in many colors.

main part of the bone, and until they have fused and ossified, reflect continued growth. Among female elephants, fusion of the epiphyses occurs around 25 years of age, whereas in males epiphyseal fusion takes place between the ages of 35 and 45. There has undoubtedly been strong selective pressure for large body size in male elephants.

Over the course of the elephants' long evolutionary history, the trend has been for increasing body size. As the Proboscideans became larger, they required stronger support for their increasing weight. The result was the evolution of legs positioned almost vertically under the body (similar to the legs of a table), rather than the angular position of most other mammals. These pillar-like legs provide strong support for their massive weight, and an elephant can doze in a standing position for long periods without expending much energy. Unlike other mammals, however, an elephant must keep at least one foot on the ground at all times. Thus, technically, an elephant cannot run, nor can it trot, canter, gallop or jump. An elephant's walk can be slow or fast; normal walking speed is about 4 mph (6 kph), but a shuffling gait of up to 25 mph (40 kph) may be attained. Compared to other animals, elephants spend a surprising amount of time walking backwards. This is because turning around requires a 'three-point-turn', and backing up for short distances uses less energy. Elephants cover an average of 15 miles (25 km) a day, but they can easily walk over 45 miles (70 km). In the desert of Namibia movements of up to 120 miles (195 km) in a day have been recorded.

Elephants are said to be the best swimmers among land dwelling mammals and they obviously enjoy playing in the water. Whole groups of elephants may gather in deep water simply to play. An elephant may disappear underwater with only the tip of its trunk, used as a snorkle, showing above the surface, and then suddenly breach like a whale, flopping on its side with a great splash. Elephants have been seen completely upside-down with only the soles of their four feet showing above the water. Babies can swim almost as soon as

Elephants walk on the tips of their fingers and toes. Inside each foot,
the digits rise to meet the wrist or heel bones. These rest on a fibrous pad, inside the
foot, which acts as a shock-absorber for the elephant's enormous weight.

A cooling mud wallow is a favorite activity for a hot day.
Vigorous kicking with the front legs and careful aim with trunkfulls of mud
can cover most of the body with mud. Sometimes simply lying down works best
and even a fully grown adult male enjoys a good wiggle in the mud.

they can walk and have been observed suckling underwater, leaving only the tip of their trunk above the surface to breathe.

The skin of an elephant may be as thick as 1 in (2.5 cm) or more on its back, head and the soles of its feet, while the skin on the posterior side of the ear, around the mouth and the anus, is paper-thin. Despite its thick, rough and bumpy appearance, the skin of an elephant is an extremely sensitive organ. For example, elephants frequently use the soles of their hind feet to examine objects or gently to wake up small calves.

The skin of both African and Asian elephants is gray in color (although some elephants are dappled with pink due to a genetic lack of pigmentation) and the range of tan, chocolate brown to ochre-colored elephants is merely a consequence of wallowing and dusting in different colored soils. Mud wallowing and dusting not only feels good but helps to protect the skin against ultraviolet radiation, insect bites and moisture loss.

One of the characteristics of modern elephants is that they have very little body hair. Sparse hair and bristles are distributed unevenly over the body, concentrated around eyes, ear openings, the chin, the trunk, and the end of the tail. The hair on the trunk, in particular, is associated with nerve endings which provide discriminatory tactile sensations.

The skin of an elephant is rough and fissured.

In comparison to other mammals elephants have a small surface area to body weight ratio, and therefore they cannot dissipate heat energy as readily. To solve the potential problem of over-heating elephants are anatomically adapted with large ears which function as heat radiators. The skin on the back side of the ears is only some $^1/_{10}$ in (2 mm) thick and is supplied with numerous blood vessels. By flapping their ears rhythmically back and forth, elephants are able to cool the circulating blood and therefore control their body temperature.

An elephant's ears also have numerous communication functions. Large, widely spaced ears are perfectly designed for listening in to distant, low-frequency sound waves, like those produced by calling elephants. And when elephants are vocalizing they typically flap their ears rapidly. The position of the ear, the type of movement, and the rate of flapping appear to be specific to the kind of call being produced, and by raising and flapping their ears elephants may be able to affect subtly the quality of the sound. Ear flapping is most vigorous during periods of social excitement when, among African elephants, secretion from the temporal glands is most noticeable. Ear flapping may also waft the odor from the temporal glands, located behind the eyes, which is used in olfactory communication, toward other elephants.

Contrary to popular belief, rhythmic ear flapping is not a signal that an elephant is angry or about to charge. There are, however, very clear ear positions and postures, such as 'ear waving' and a particular kind of 'ear folding', that are part of an elephant's threat repertoire, and other elephants (and humans) ignore these messages at their peril! A silent charge with ears folded, trunk curled under, and head down is far more serious than the Hollywood mock charge typified by loud trumpets, head and tusks high, ears extended, and trunk outstretched. On the other hand, an ear fold associated with ears raised high, loud screaming, trumpeting and rumbling, though initially terrifying, is merely an elephant's greeting ceremony. Just as young elephants must learn to read ear language, so anyone who works with elephants must learn to understand their signals.

In their lifetime Asian and African elephants have 26 teeth which include

Elephant's eyes, small but wise, are the color of old amber.

two upper incisors, the tusks, 12 deciduous premolars and 12 molars. Once again elephants are an exception, as they do not replace teeth in a vertical manner (i.e. from above or below) as most mammals do, but rather in a horizontal progression. A newborn elephant has two to three teeth in each quadrant and, as it ages, new, bigger teeth develop from behind, slowly moving forward to replace these. As these bigger teeth come into wear they continue to move forward, eventually fragmenting, bit by bit, at the anterior edge and falling out of the mouth, or being swallowed. The timing and rate of tooth replacement is similar for both elephant species. The first teeth are replaced at 2–3 years old, the second at 4–6 years, the third at 12–15 years, the fourth at around 25–30 years and the fifth at 40–45. The sixth molar comes into full wear at about 43 years old and must last the elephant for the rest of its life.

Elephant tusks are composed mostly of dentine and, in cross-section, exhibit a unique pattern of lines that criss-cross one another in a zigzag or diamond shaped pattern. It is this pattern that makes elephant ivory unique. Elephants are born with deciduous incisors, or milk tusks, and these are replaced by permanent tusks within 6–12 months of birth. In African elephants these small growing tusks first show beyond the elephant's lip at approximately 18 months for males and closer to two years for females. Tusks then grow continuously at a rate of approximately 7 in (17 cm) per year, though the tusks of male African elephants apparently grow even faster late in life.

Typically, only two-thirds of the tusk is visible, the rest being embedded in the socket within the cranium. An elephant's tusks, as with all mammalian teeth, have pulp cavities containing highly vascularized tissues innervated by fine nerve branches making them sensitive to external pressure.

Both male and female African elephants carry tusks, although the rate of tusklessness is always higher among females. The degree of tusklessness among

Tusks are a useful resting place for a 300 lb (136 kg) nose.

females varies from one population to the next, from less than 2% to 15% or more. To a large extent tusklessness reflects the degree of ivory exploitation the population has undergone. In heavily poached populations where hunters select tusked elephants, as many as 40% of the large adult females are tuskless. Since tusklessness is hereditary, these populations have witnessed an increasing proportion of tuskless young elephants in recent years. Among Asian elephants the tusks of females are vestigial (present in the socket,

Males in full musth secrete a viscous liquid from enlarged temporal glands, located behind the eyes, and leave a trail of strong-smelling urine. High ranking males lose as much as 63 gal (240 liters) of urine in 24 hours.

but not visible below the lip) or totally absent, and tuskless males, known as 'mukhna', are much more common. The tusks of Asian elephants are considerably shorter and lighter than those of African elephants. The longest recorded tusks for an African elephant measured 10.7 ft (3.26 m), and the heaviest weighed 226.4 lb (102.7 kg). By comparison the record length for an Asian elephant is 9.9 ft (3.02 m) and the record weight only 86 lb (39 kg).

Among African elephants there is strong sexual dimorphism in tusk weight. The tusks of males grow exponentially with age, and by 55 years old the tusks of males are seven times the weight of the tusks of females. The average tusk weight of a 55-year-old male is 108 lb (49 kg) per tusk, while the average tusk weight of a female of the same age is a mere 15 lb (7 kg) per tusk. It is the very much larger tusks of males that have made them so

*Jezebel, a famous matriarch with long, asymmetrical tusks,
leads her family across Kenya's Amboseli plains.*

*Elephants are highly social animals; here Asian
elephants gather in a forest habitat for the act of dusting.*

vulnerable to ivory poachers. In many populations of elephants in Africa today most of the mature males over 40 years old have been killed, and the sex ratio of breeding adults is highly skewed toward females. The much thicker tusks of mature males creates an 'hour-glass' shaped face (broad foreheads, narrowing below the eyes and widening again at the tusk sockets), and this feature, in combination with the relatively larger heads of males, clearly distinguishes the two sexes at a glance.

Tusks are multipurpose instruments and are used by elephants to dig for water, minerals, and roots. They are very useful for prying bark off trees, breaking branches, or as levers for maneuvering felled trees. Elephants typically favor a particular tusk when handling food and years of use produces a deep groove which eventually breaks off. Tusks are important for both sexes in display and defense, and they are a matter of life and death for battling males. Domesticated elephants use their tusks for work, and all elephants with tusks use them as trunk rests.

It is the elephant's trunk that makes the Proboscidea truly unique. A fusion of the nose and the upper lip, the trunk has at its tip two openings which are, of course, the nostrils. But an elephant's trunk has far more uses than merely breathing. It is a highly sensitive organ equipped with an estimated 150,000 muscle units. At once a terrifically strong, and yet highly tactile and sensitive appendage, an elephant's trunk is, in many ways, more versatile than a human hand. It is used by elephants to eat and drink, to mudsplash and dust, to comfort and reassure, to lift and push, to fight and play, to attack and defend, to smell and vocalize. An elephant's trunk is, quite simply, indispensable. With this extraordinary number of uses it is hard to comprehend why such an appendage has not evolved in more than just the Proboscidea.

Using its trunk an elephant can push over a tree or pick up an object $\frac{1}{10}$ in (0.25 cm) in diameter. By flicking the tip of its trunk gently back and forth in a pool of water an elephant cleans dirt and floating vegetation away before drinking. By sucking water into its trunk an elephant can pour some 16 pints (9 liters) of water into its mouth at a time. An elephant is able to cover almost its entire body in a cooling mud bath, by careful aim of a trunkful of mud. By blowing through its trunk as it tosses dust on itself, an elephant is able to spread the powder evenly.

An elephant uses its trunk to rub itchy eyes or ears. And if the inside of its trunk has an itch, an elephant places the bothersome nostril over the tip of a tusk and twists it back and forth. A female elephant uses her trunk to reach back and touch a suckling baby, to calm one that is frightened or to pull one out of harm's way. An elephant greets a non-relative by placing its trunk in the other's mouth. An elephant uses its trunk to smell danger, to detect a female in estrus from several miles away, to track a rival male, and to recognize the urine or temporal gland secretion of members of its own family. By holding its trunk in different positions an elephant communicates with others, and by blowing through its trunk an elephant can produce a variety of different trumpets and snorts.

In the study of elephant behavior the position of an elephant's trunk is highly informative. The tip of the trunk is almost never stationary, moving in whatever direction the elephant finds interesting. An elephant's attention is usually stimulated by what other elephants are doing, and observing the trunk tip is a clue to both subtle behavior that is occurring or an interaction that is about to take place. An elephant's trunk and tusks are its most useful tools and many an elephant has learned that tusks do not conduct electricity and can be used to break electric fence wires. Elephants have been known intentionally to throw or drop large rocks and logs on the live wires of electric fences, either breaking the wire or loosening it so that it makes contact with the earth wire, thus shorting the fence.

Some tusks lend themselves for draping a trunk, others for tucking.

Elephants also use tools that they find in their environment. Elephants will hold a stick in their trunk and use it to remove a tick from between their forelegs. They may pick up a palm frond or similar piece of vegetation and use it as a fly swat to reach a part of the body that the trunk cannot. Elephants may pick up objects in their environments and throw them, under trunk, at their enemies or playmates with surprising accuracy.

Elephants are considered among the most intelligent of non-human animals. Perhaps, as in humans where the development of the brain paralleled the evolution of upright posture and the freeing of a dextrous hand for tool use, the complexity of an elephant's brain may be related to the use of its trunk.

Although the elephant's brain is small relative to its body size, weighing between 9 and 13 lb (4 and 6 kg), the cerebrum and cerebellum are highly convoluted. The temporal lobes of the cerebrum, which in humans function as the memory storage area, are very large, bulging out from the sides of the brain. Another measure of intelligence is the size of the brain at birth relative to its full adult size, which is considered to be an indication of the degree of learning a species undergoes during childhood. Among the majority of mammals this value is close to 90%. In humans the brain at birth is a mere 28% of its full adult size which, it has been argued, partly reflects the mechanical constraints of birth, but also indicates the long period of learning and social development that we undergo. Chimpanzees, our closest relatives, are born with 54% of their adult brain size. Elephants, too, are strikingly different from the majority of mammals with their brains at birth being only 35% of their full adult size, which in part must reflect the long period of dependency (about ten years) and learning (over 17 years) that young elephants go through. Intelligence is very difficult to measure, especially in a species whose senses are so different from our own, but certainly elephants are intelligent by non-human standards.

The Search for Food

An elephant's wide, flat teeth are perfectly designed for grinding the coarse plant material that makes up a large portion of its diet. Elephants feed in bulk, and, unlike ruminant herbivores such as buffaloes or antelopes, their fermentation chamber is in the hindgut (an enlarged caecum and colon) which is fairly inefficient at digesting plant fiber. Feeding may occupy from 60% to 70% of an elephant's waking hours; in the process of selective feeding an adult male may consume around 310 lb (140 kg) of wet forage in an average 24 hour period. An adult elephant may drink as much as 50 gallons (225 liters) of water a day. They can go without water for up to four days, but will will drink several times a day if water is available.

Elephants eat grass, reeds, shrubs, herbs, creepers, trees, leaves, twigs, shoots, branches, thorns, succulent plants, bark, flowers, fruit pods, seeds, roots, and tubers. Each species of plant is handled in a specific way by using a variety of complex trunk, mouth, tusk, and foot movements. For example, with the two separate lobes or fingers on the end of its trunk, an African elephant can pluck individual leaves, flowers, or fruits from plants. Elephants can strip bunches of leaves from a branch, pull up a clump of grass, pick up fallen fruit from the ground, and can dig up roots, stolons, bulbs and tubers with sharp-edged toenails, trunk and tusks working together.

In general, elephants prefer high-quality grasses to woody plants because they have fewer chemical defenses and are easier to digest. Browse is, however, extremely important for nutritional balance. In open rangeland elephants feed mostly on grass during the wet season, when it is of high quality and in plentiful supply, and turn increasingly to browse as the dry season progresses. The diet of elephants living in woodlands and forests

A mature male has a deep scratch on a favorite rubbing tree.

contains more browse, but many studies have shown that grass is often taken in a higher proportion than its availability. Elephants living in forests feed extensively on fruit and, hence, are important seed dispersers.

With their enormous appetites and ability to consume almost all parts of the plants in their habitats, elephants have an almost unique potential, perhaps second only to man, for modifying their own environment dramatically over relatively short time scales. The changes in habitat caused by densities of elephants can affect other species, in extreme cases causing local extinction. Habitat change may even affect the elephants themselves, and when the food supply becomes depleted, they may move on or suffer reproductive failure or higher mortality. When elephants disappear from a savannah environment, the consequences may be marked and significant; places that were once grasslands supporting large populations of plains grazers and their predators become dense thickets with a lower biomass of predominantly browsing antelopes.

In many parts of Africa, the elephants have congregated in parks and reserves to avoid human encroachment and ivory poaching and this has led to conspicuous transformations in habitats. In such cases, wildlife managers may wish to take action to arrest these changes, such as manipulating water supplies and elephant distributions, fencing off patches of woodland, moving elephants elsewhere or simply shooting them to reduce local density. However, tropical environments are very dynamic and resilient in the face of disturbance. Woodlands may come and go, and come back yet again, in cycles which are regular or erratic and may take decades to unfold. It is important to take a large-scale perspective when we look at the balance between the state of the environment and the largest of land animals, and to harness both our imagination and our compassion when deciding what, if anything, needs to be done.

Elephants occupy a keystone position in the community of herbivores.

The Lives of the Two Sexes

Elephant social organization is usually described as being matriarchal, that is, a society in which families are led by females. While this is true, the label ignores male society, and theirs is equally fascinating. Perhaps the most fundamental behavioral difference between male and female elephants is that adult females and their dependent offspring live in tight-knit stable family groups, while adult males live more solitary, independent lives with few social bonds. Let us start where each elephant begins its life, with the family unit.

An elephant family is typically composed of several related females and their offspring. A family may be as small as two individuals, a mother and her calf, or as large as 40 or more individuals, including great-grandmothers, their daughters, their granddaughters, their great-granddaughters and their immature sons. Usually the oldest and largest adult female assumes the role of matriarch, and her leadership is both dramatic and pivotal when the family or an individual member faces danger or is in crisis. Contrary, however, to conventional wisdom, all adults participate in mundane decision making through a process of suggestion, negotation and consensus. The matriarch's role is gained through respect, not through force, and her extraordinary role of defender, reconciler and leader is obvious in the subtle deference of family members to her authority and her wishes. The bonds of the family radiate around her, and her death may cause a family to split up.

The size of an elephant family depends on many factors, but generally, families tend to be smaller in forest, woodland or bushland habitats, and larger in grassland ecosystems. This is because in grasslands individuals can remain in large close-knit groups and still obtain enough food, whereas in forests the habitat requires an individual to be more selective and thus inter-individual

With mouth wide open and ears flapping a mother calls to a member of her family.

THE COLLEGE OF WEST ANGLIA

distance must be greater. Within each of these habitats, however, larger and smaller families will occur, and the size of families is influenced by both the reproductive and survival success of individuals within the family as well as the strength of the friendships between the adult females.

There are many benefits associated with belonging to a large family. Larger families with older matriarchs tend to be dominant to smaller families with younger matriarchs, and are thus able to compete more successfully for scarce resources. Calves born into large families with more female caretakers are more likely to survive than calves born into smaller families.

Belonging to a large family is not the only way to obtain some of these benefits because the bonds of a female elephant extend out beyond the family in a series of multi-tiered relationships, through bond groups and clans. Bond groups are made up of one to five closely allied families that are usually related, and often result from the fission of family units. Above the level of the bond group is the clan, which has been defined as families that use the same dry season home range.

Elephants tend to aggregate during and immediately following the rainy seasons, when food is well distributed and plentiful. In African savannahs families may gather together in aggregations numbering several hundred individuals and over a thousand elephants have been observed in these wet-season gatherings. As the dry season progresses, the groups begin to split up. Apart from all the biological arguments that have been used to explain these congregations, such as breeding and survival benefits, it appears that elephants just plain enjoy being together, and will be if they can be. Interactions between females, both within and between families, are generally amicable except when there is competition over a scarce resource, such as food, water or minerals.

The size and structure of groups that a female elephant finds herself in depend upon a number of different social and environmental factors which include: the basic size of her family unit; the number of individuals making up

*Waterholes are important gathering places for elephants and the focus
of intense social behavior. As groups of elephants come and go, it is easy for a trained eye
to pick out the matriarch of each family and to discern which groups are related.*

During sexually inactive periods male elephants retire to bull areas where they interact in a relaxed and amiable manner. Males continue to grow through most of their lives and dominance is based on body size.

her bond group; the strength of bonds between her own and other families; the habitat type; the season; and, in many cases, the level of human threat.

Females become sexually mature and come into their first estrus anywhere from 8 to 18 years old depending on habitat quality and food availability. Gestation is an average 660 days long and females give birth to their first calf at anywhere from 10 to 20 years of age. Thereafter, depending upon food availability, females produce a calf on average every 4 to 6 years, slowing down as they approach 50 years old but often continuing into their sixties.

At birth, newborn elephants are welcomed into this tightly knit society by the loud roaring and rumbling of their older relatives. A pair of breasts, which look extraordinarily like those of a human female, are located between the mother's forelegs, more similar to the primates than to most other mammals. Newborns are able to stand within an hour and have their first suck of milk soon after. Young calves suck frequently (about every half hour for young males and every 50 minutes for females) and do not begin to feed on their own until they are around four months old. Calves continue to suckle until they are between four and six years old, and even eight-year-olds have been known to get down on their front wrists for a drink of milk. Typically calves are weaned, amidst very loud protests, when their mother is in late pregnancy with her next calf.

Techniques such as drinking, feeding, mudsplashing, dusting, and manipulating objects must be learned by young elephants. The amount of practice a young elephant needs to master the many uses of its extraordinary trunk is merely one dimension of the long period of learning elephants experience. It can be argued that the period of dependency for a young elephant is as long as that of a human child. Babies who are orphaned under the age of two do not survive their mother's death. Between the ages of two and five, up to 70% die in the two years following their mother's death, and between five and ten, 50% will die. Not only must survival and social techniques be learned but there is a strong emotional attachment between a calf and its mother. Anyone who has tried to raise an orphaned baby elephant will say that the first task is to help the calf overcome its grief.

Learning continues through the teenage years, and mothers have been observed leading their teenage daughters to the 'proper' mate, and guiding her through the steps of courtship. As with humans, teenagers do not usually make the best mothers (calf mortality is significantly higher among young mothers) and their offspring seem to know. Though they are suckled by their mothers, many babies of young mothers spend a large portion of their time with their grand-mothers.

The survival of females and their offspring depends upon the cohesion and co-ordination of the extended family, and on their ability to compete with other groups for access to scarce resources. It is not suprising, therefore, that these very social mammals have a large vocal repertoire. The vocal communcation of African elephants has been studied in more detail than that of Asian elephants. Family members use calls to reinforce bonds between relatives and friends, to care for youngsters, to reconcile differences between friends, to form coalitions against aggressors, and to keep in contact with one another over long distances.

African elephants emit a broad range of sounds, from low-frequency rumbles to higher-frequency trumpets, roars, screams, bellows, cries, barks and snorts, as well as some idiosyncratic sounds made up by individuals. In all some 60 different calls are known. Many calls are typically emitted in chorus with other elephants. The rumbles are the most numerous (30 known) and complex class of calls. All of the rumbles contain components below the level of human hearing, with some being totally infrasonic.

Elephant rumbles are harmonic sounds. In other words, they contain frequencies that are multiples of the lowest or fundamental frequency. While the fundamental frequency is typically inaudiable to human ears, at least some

All family members help to take care of youngsters. This one-year-old baby has raised his ears in alarm. His distress call would bring relatives, young and old, rushing to his side with rumbles of reassurance and comforting touching with their trunks.

of the upper harmonics are usually within the audible range. Some calls are extraordinarily powerful and the lowest frequencies may be heard by other elephants up to 5 to10 kilometers away. Recent research suggests that elephants also transmit these and other powerful signals through the ground, or seismically, over at least double these distances. Although it now seems that elephants do make use of seismic communication, there is some debate about how they do it. One theory is that vibrations conducted through their skeletons may stimulate their exceptionally large middle-ear bones. We also know that they have specialized cells that are vibrationally sensitive in their trunks and feet.

As a consequence of their highly social nature and their ability to communicate over long distances, elephants have an unusually extensive network of vocal recognition. It has been estimated that adult females are able to recognise the individual voices of at least 100 other adult females. While females use many different vocalisations in active communcation within and between family groups, males use many fewer calls, relying instead on listening to locate groups of females. Male elephants live a more solitary life, where reproductive success and survival depend to a degree upon an individual's ability to detect sounds made by others, and by advertising their sexual state, identify and rank.

If the only knowledge we had about elephants was tape recordings of their calls by sex and by age, we would immediately be struck by how apparently different the concerns of the two sexes are. Far from the supportive family life, adult males are on their own, living in a dynamic world where body size and condition, sexual state, dominance rank, and detailed knowledge of your rivals are what count. Male elephants leave their nurturing, closely bonded natal families at about 14 years old and must begin the task of learning a whole new set of rules that will then govern the rest of their lives. How do young males make this transition?

Sparring allows males to reassess the size and strength of their age mates.

Starting in the first year of life, male play is already noticeably rougher than that of females. By the age of four, when young females are helping to take care of younger babies, males are spending more time away from their mother's side, engaged in rough play with other young males. They are beginning the process of what will determine their success and even their survival as an adult: learning the characteristics of their age mates, and acquiring the ability to size up their rivals. From around the age of eight or nine years old males begin to spend some time away from the family, usually joining another family for a few days before returning. By an average age of 14 males have usually left their families.

At this young age they are still smaller than a fully grown adult female and less than half the weight of a large adult male. And, while they are growing, they still have much to learn. As the older males go about their business, searching for estrous females, mating and fighting, it is entertaining to observe teenage males tagging along behind, watching their mentors. In a subordinate, head low posture they will stand near or follow an older male, investigating each spot of urine that the older male has sniffed. The older males are gentle with these youngsters since, of course, at this age they pose no competition.

Male African elephants reach sexual maturity (that is the production of sperm in significant quantity) at about 17 years old. But at this age a young male is still only a little over half of his adult size, and cannot begin to compete with older males for access to mates. Although young males in their early twenties begin to try to mount estrous females, they are unlikely to be successful for several reasons. In natural populations there are many older, larger, more experienced males, and they work hard to ensure that younger males do not steal their mate. Even if they do have the opportunity to mate, the act itself takes a bit of practice. Unlike most other mammals, elephants have a highly mobile S-shaped penis and they do not thrust. It takes a young male a few years of practice to gain sufficient control over his penis to insert it successfully into

*In the first year of life a mother elephant keeps a very close watch on
her baby, waking him up when it is time to go, and checking that he is still behind her
by touching him gently with her hind foot and with a swish of her tail.*

Two musth males battle for supremacy.
Fights occur between musth males of equal fighting
ability and may end in injury or death.

a female's vagina. Once this has been achieved they have yet another major obstacle: females prefer to be mated by older males, and when mounted by a small male they simply take several steps forward, causing the male to fall off.

Once a male has reached his mid twenties he begins to show distinct sexually active and inactive periods. During sexually inactive periods males spend time alone or in small groups of other males in particular bull areas, where interactions are relaxed and amicable. During sexually active periods, males leave their bull areas and move in search of estrous females.

Then one day, during the height of a sexually active period, a male begins to exhibit a marked increase in aggression. His temporal glands, located behind his eyes, begin to secrete a viscous liquid, and urine begins to dribble from his penis. He has entered his first musth. The word musth comes from the Urdu, *mast*, meaning intoxicated in a sexual sense, and refers to a heightened period of sexual and aggressive activity, or rut. During musth, males secrete a viscous liquid from swollen temporal glands, leave a trail of strong smelling urine and call repeatedly in very low frequencies. Testosterone (the male hormone that controls sexual and aggressive behavior) rises dramatically above its non-musth level, and behavior becomes extremely aggressive toward other males, particularly toward those in musth.

Musth has been documented for centuries in domesticated Asian elephants because its occurrence caused such interruptions to the work schedule. Some of the historical documents written by the owners of working elephants are fascinating. Daily rationing of food and water was used to prevent the onset of musth, and if it was too late for prevention, remedies to minimize an elephant's rage included huge doses of Epsom salts or opium. In a book written in 1901 on the treatment of elephant diseases, G.H. Evans advised the following to calm a musth male's excitement:

> Four to six drachmas of opium or ganja [marijuana] given with boiled
> rice, plantains or jaggery; or three drachmas of camphor and two of

opium twice a day for two days; or eight pounds each of wheat flour, onions, and sugar and four pounds of ghee [clarified butter], mixed together and worked into orange-sized pills and administered one each night and morning until the whole is taken.

According to Evans, after this treatment most animals would carry on their work as usual.

For many years it was believed that musth did not occur in African elephants, and it was less than 20 years ago that it was first documented in the African genus. It is ironic that today more is known about the phenomenon among free living elephants in Africa than in Asia. Musth appears to be almost identical in the two genera, and the only significant difference seems to be that Asian elephants come into musth at a slightly younger age. Most of these cases, however, occur in captivity where there is little or no suppression of musth by the presence of older, larger males. Among wild African elephants the occurrence of musth in younger males is strongly influenced by the proximity of older musth males. For example, a young male may come into musth within an hour of encountering an unguarded estrous female, but be forced out of musth immediately following an attack by a higher ranking musth male.

Among young males the duration of musth is short and sporadic, while the musth periods of older males last several months and occur at a predictable time each year. The highest ranking males in a population come into musth during and following the rains when females are in bigger groups and the greatest number are likely to come into estrous. As a consequence of continued growth in height and body weight, larger, older males rank above smaller, younger males and thus male elephants do not reach their sexual prime until they are 45 years old. These older males are successful not only because of their large size, but because females actively choose to mate with them

Elephants enjoy water from a very young age.

Elephants and Humans

The relationship between elephants and man is and has been an extraordinary one. We view elephants with a degree of respect and fondness that we reserve for few other creatures on earth. And yet, however much our affinity for elephants, our relationship with them has always been an exploitative one. Elephants have been hunted for meat and for ivory, killed for raiding our crops, captured for domestication, trained for carrying out tasks and for performing in circuses or religious ceremonies.

Elephants were first tamed in the Indus Valley about 2000 BC and were used for a range of chores. Today there are between 13,000 and 16,500 working elephants in Asia, making up 25% of the entire Asian elephant population. Elephants are employed to carry tourists in national parks, to haul loads, to pull logs out of forests, to capture wild elephants, to lead religious ceremonies and to assist in many other activities that require strength and intelligence. The qualities said to make elephants so useful, in comparison with machinery, include their intelligence, flexibility (they can work almost anywhere from in water to dense forest, to steep hillsides), low maintenance costs, and minimal impact on the environment. It is common for elephants to know over 30 commands although, apparently, they don't always wait to be told. They seem to understand what is expected of them and if something is out of place they will often rectify it of their own volition. Many people who work with elephants argue that they have reasoned thought. For example, domesticated elephants have been known to stuff mud into the bells around their necks to muffle them before they go out into the neighboring farms to steal bananas.

Elephants have also been used in war, and the first record of an elephant killed in battle dates back to 1100 BC in the Indus Valley. Elephants were

An Asian elephant is given a daily bath by her mahout.

trained either to pass the enemy up to their mahouts, who would dispatch him, or to hold the enemy down with the trunk or foreleg while impaling him with a tusk. Porus, Emperor of India, used 85 elephants to confront Alexander the Great at the Battle of Hydaspes in 326 BC. And Ptolemy, one of Alexander's generals, imported Indian elephants to Egypt. African elephants, too, were used in battle and when Ptolemy's elephants aged and died, his son, Ptolemy II, ensured a steady supply by capturing wild African elephants. The use of war elephants spread across North Africa and into the peninsula of Greece where in 280 BC King Pyrrhus invaded Italy with 20 elephants, causing the Roman horses to panic. Hannibal transported a corps of 37 African elephants through southern Spain and France and across the Alps to invade Italy in 218 BC. Though his invasion was daringly conceived and brilliantly executed most of his elephants eventually succumbed to disease.

In modern times, too, African elephants have been trained. In 1879 the Belgian king, Leopold II, attempted to bring four Asian elephants to the Congo but all died on the way. Twenty years later he attempted to catch wild African elephant calves by first shooting the mother and then sending men running after the frightened calf, looping one end of a rope around its leg and the other end around a tree. By 1913 there were 33 elephants in captivity at the Elephant Domestication Center, and the elephants were eventually trained to work in agriculture and forestry. The Center still exists today in the Garamba National Park in the Democratic Republic of Congo (formerly Zaire), where elephants are used for taking tourists on game rides. Elephant-back safaris are also available in the Okavango Delta, Botswana, and a number of other elephant safari centers are starting up around the continent.

Sadly the most common interaction between man and elephants today is one of conflict. There are simply too many people and expanding agriculture is encroaching on most elephant habitats. The single biggest threat to the future survival of elephants is the shrinking habitat available to them. Within

our own recorded history elephants formed an almost continuous series of populations from Africa to China. We have whittled them down to two main groups, African and Asian elephants, which are now separated by several thousand miles.

Asian elephants were once distributed from Syria and Iraq to China and south to Sumatra. Throughout history Asian elephants have disappeared where forests have been cleared for human needs. Today their distribution is very fragmented and elephants occur only in small populations in India, Sri Lanka, Nepal, Bhutan, Bangladesh, Myanmar (formerly Burma), China, Thailand, Laos, Cambodia, Vietnam, Malaysia and Indonesia. The total Asian elephant population is estimated at fewer than 44,000 individuals, and loss of habitat is the cause of the elephant's declining numbers and its endangered status. Exploding human populations have turned crucial elephant habitats into farmland and eliminated traditional migratory routes; slash and burn agriculture has destroyed large sections of forest, fragmenting populations and making the long-term survival of elephants in many areas unlikely. As agriculture expands and elephant habitat shrinks, conflict between people and elephants can only increase. In India alone between 200 and 300 people are killed by elephants each year. In most countries there is little future for the Asian elephant except in a few protected areas.

Ancient historical writings document the occurrence of African elephants in North Africa as far as the Mediterranean coast. And, within the last five decades, African elephants inhabited all sub-Saharan Africa except for extremely arid areas. Today, though elephants still exist in 34 African countries, their range is fragmented and populations are becoming increasingly isolated.

While habitat loss has primarily accounted for the decrease in Asian elephant numbers, the quest for ivory can be held responsible for the decline of

There is so little space left for elephants.

Between 1979 and 1989 over half a million African elephants were illegally killed to meet the world's demand for ivory. In 1989 Kenya burned its ivory stockpile in a clear statement that the trade should be banned; it was, later that year, with dramatic and positive results. The 1997 decision to reopen a limited trade in ivory sends a mistaken green light to consumers, and an ominous message to elephants. Mutilated carcasses may once again become a common sight in Africa's national parks.

the African elephant. Ivory is a beautiful substance, coveted by humans for at least the last 25,000 years. The oldest ivory sculpture, the *Venus of Landes*, was found in a cave in France, and dates from the Upper Palaeolithic. All the great ancient civilizations of Asia, Europe and Africa prized elephant ivory, and ivory carving centers dating from before 3000 BC have been uncovered in Babylon.

The demand for ivory has continued throughout human history, and indications are that it was primarily pressure from ivory hunting which caused the extinction of elephants in North Africa in the Middle Ages. Excessive hunting in the eighteenth and nineteenth centuries brought elephants in southern Africa to the brink of extinction, and a similar rush for ivory took place in West Africa, peaking in the nineteenth and early twentieth centuries, from which populations have never recovered. The rapid decline of the elephants across sub-Saharan Africa during the eighteenth and nineteenth centuries was closely linked with the slave trade, as slave caravans were used to transport tusk to the coast from the interior.

The message: do not sell, buy, or wear ivory.

Protective legislation and a fall in the price of ivory during the first three-quarters of this century allowed many populations to recover. But by the 1970s the killing of elephants for ivory was, once again, having a serious impact on populations across most of the African continent. The paradox was that while elephants were undergoing a significant continental decline, certain populations within protected areas were locally overabundant and judged in need of culling. Many people argued that if elephants were to be legally killed then ivory should be legally traded. The problem was that by the mid 1980s, 80% of the tusks in trade were actually from illegally killed elephants. In 1979 the continental population estimate was 1.3 million elephants, and by 1989 the figure was 609,000; over half of Africa's elephants had been killed during the decade. Finally, in 1989, based on these and other alarming statistics, the Convention on International Trade in Endangered Species of Fauna and Flora (CITES) banned the international trade in ivory. The effect of the ivory trade ban was an immediate drop in the price of ivory across most of Africa and a dramatic decline in the level of poaching. Since then the ban on the trade has been relaxed in a few countries and the consequences of this decision are still being debated.

Unfortunately, ivory poaching is but one of the problems threatening the survival of the African elephant. In most areas where they now live human populations are growing at rates of between 3% and 4% per annum. Traditional elephant habitat is being carved up for agriculture and elephants are increasingly being confined in parks and reserves, which are often too small to support them year round. As individuals try to move beyond their boundaries they meet opposition from farmers. A common solution is to fence most elephants inside protected areas, and to shoot any that come into conflict with people outside. But in many places land-hungry people are encroaching upon the protected forests, parks and reserves that have been set aside for elephants.

The earth's elephants are under threat and although our generation will not witness the last of these extraordinary creatures, ours may be the generation that decides their fate. Will we stand by and watch as the remaining elephants are killed by ivory poachers, shot for raiding crops, or fenced into small protected areas to be culled on a regular basis? Or will we have the imagination and the courage to find a better way to live with elephants?

What will their future be?

African Elephant Facts

Scientific name	*Loxodonta africana*	Interbirth interval	4–6 years
Ave. max height (male)	almost 13 ft (4 m)	Age at first musth	average 29 years
		Longevity	60–70 years
Ave. max height (female)	just under 9 ft (2.7 m)	Skin	wrinkled
		Shape of back	concave
Ave. max weight (male)	over 13,200 lb (6000 kg)	Teeth	lozenge-shaped loops
Ave. max weight (female)	6100 lb (2767 kg)	Tusks	both sexes
		Tip of trunk	two finger
Ave. weight newborn	265 lb (120 kg)	Ave. max tusk weight (male)	108 lb (49 kg)
Age at first reproduction	8–18 years	Ave. max tusk weight (female)	15 lb (7 kg)
Gestation	660 days		

Asian Elephant Facts

Scientific name	*Elephas maximus*	Longevity	60–70 years
Ave. max height (male)	up to 11.5 ft (3.5 m)	Skin	smoother
		Shape of back	convex
Ave. max weight (male)	up to 12,125 lb (5500 kg)	Teeth	narrow compressed loops
Ave. weight newborn	165–253 lb (75–115 kg)	Tusks	females tuskless
Age at first reproduction	8–13 years	Tip of trunk	one finger
		Ave. max tusk weight (female)	usually vestigial or absent
Gestation	about 660 days		
Interbirth interval	4–6 years		

Index

Recommended Reading

Chadwick, D, *The Fate of the Elephant*, London, 1993.

Douglas-Hamilton, I & O., *Battle for the Elephants*, London, 1992.

Moss, C. J. *Elephant Memories*, New York, 1988.

Poole, Joyce, J. *Coming of Age with Elephants*, New York, 1996.

Shoshani, J. *Elephants: Majestic Creatures of the Wild*, Sydney, 1992.

Sukumar, R. *The Asian Elephant: Ecology and Management*, Cambridge, 1989.

The Author

Joyce Poole received her Ph.D in animal behavior from Cambridge University and completed her post-doctoral training at Princeton University. She spent 14 years studying the elephants at Amboseli National Park, her research there focusing on the sexual and aggressive behavior of musth males and vocal communication of females. In the early 1990s Joyce headed Kenya's elephant conservation and management programme.